THE GREAT
RACEHORSES

THE GREAT
RACEHORSES

JULIAN WILSON

LITTLE, BROWN AND COMPANY
BOSTON NEW YORK LONDON

A LITTLE, BROWN BOOK

First published by Queen Anne Press in 1987

This revised edition published in Great Britain in 1998
by Little, Brown and Company (UK)

All pedigrees supplied by Eclipse Pedigrees, Weatherbys

A CIP catalogue record for this book is available from the British Library

ISBN 0-316-64468-4

10 9 8 7 6 5 4 3 2 1

Picture Credits

Ackermann Gallery: 62, 162, 175 COLOUR St Simon
Allsport: 35, 112
Associated Press: 38
Blood Horse, Kentucky: 70–71, 93, 102, 120, 139, 172, 187
Bridgeman Art Library: COLOUR Carbine
Gerry Cranham: 14, 16, 46, 56, 97, 104, 129, 142, 191, 193, 216, 229, 232
    COLOUR Arkle, Crisp, Mill House, Mill Reef, Oh So Sharp, Red Rum
Sue Crawford: COLOUR Park Top (by kind permission of the Duke of Devonshire), Ribot
Hulton Getty Picture Library: 20, 26, 40, 67, 153, 177, 200, 247
Illustrated London News: 54, 115, 170
Jockey Club/Colour Laboratory: 157 COLOUR Eclipse, Nijinsky, Sun Chariot
Jockey Club/Laurie Morton: COLOUR Sir Ivor
Jockey Club/Tryon Gallery: COLOUR Touchstone
Mansell Collection: 50, 69, 74, 107, 124, 133
Peter Ohlson: 48
Photo Source: 166
Popperfoto: 42
W. W. Rouch: 18, 24, 31, 33, 52, 65, 75, 81, 88, 90, 95, 100, 117, 133, 145,
    155, 204, 213, 221, 226, 241, 253, 255 COLOUR Brigadier Gerard
George Selwyn: 78, 197, 235, 249, 251 COLOUR Night Nurse, Monksfield, Shergar
Sport and General: 12, 22, 28, 59, 64, 83, 109, 126, 137, 151, 159, 164, 168,
    182, 184, 189, 202, 208, 210, 239, 244

Design by The Bridgewater Book Company Limited

PRINTED IN ITALY

LITTLE, BROWN AND COMPANY (UK)
Brettenham House
Lancaster Place
London WC2E 7EN

CONTENTS

INTRODUCTION

How to compare generations? It remains an ageless argument in sport. Was Dixie Dean a greater goalscorer than Alan Shearer? Was Compton a finer batsman than Lara? Was Ormonde a greater racehorse than Mill Reef?

No sport remains static. In football, defences are better disciplined – thanks to contemporary coaching – and the modern game is far faster. In cricket, bowling is more hostile, and playing surfaces often less predictable, because of covered wickets. In racing, there are now upwards of 8000 runners on the Flat in Britain each year, many with the finest international pedigrees, and British racing remains the most competitive in the world. In Ormonde's era there were just 2000 runners, almost all owner-bred by the British landed gentry.

So, how to compare the champions of the nineteenth century and the early twentieth century with the multi-million pound 'superstars' of today? The task has been both intriguing and speculative. Historical 'evidence' is often confusing. The contemporary wordsmith who claimed that Eclipse (1764) could 'run a mile in a minute' had a clearly questionable method of timing. (The present course record at Newmarket is 1 minute 35.08 seconds.)

The style of riding, as evidenced by the classic paintings of the nineteenth century, was in total contrast to today's 'crouch' and races would usually become a sprint over two or three furlongs. But horses in general were tougher, more durable and harder-trained. Future generations will have the benefit of television recordings to evaluate the achievements of the champions of today. We can only speculate on the giants of old.

The post-war popularity of National Hunt racing has resulted in the second part of this book being devoted to jumpers. The Grand National apart, top-class hurdle racing and steeplechasing is a relatively modern phenomenon. For instance, the value of the Champion Hurdle and Cheltenham Gold Cup in the 1930s was a mere £670. For this reason there are, in the author's opinion, fewer jumpers worthy of the epithet 'great' than flat-race champions, tracing back to Eclipse. Hence the ratio of 70/30 in favour of Flat Racing.

Inevitably there will be criticisms of any personal selection. The Irish will question how Vincent O'Brien's triple Gold Cup winner, Cottage Rake, can be excluded, and a relatively modest steeplechaser, Aldaniti, included. The answer is that there is more than one gate to greatness. Modern racegoers would argue that Bosra Sham, at her peak, would have defeated Oh So Sharp; that Generous was superior to Grundy. Other omissions sure to offend are, on the Flat: Abernant, Blue Peter, Djebel, Fairway, Pinza, Quashed and Tetratema; and under National Hunt Rules: Poethlyn, Freebooter, Gregalach, Kellsborough Jack and National Spirit.

A further problem for the racing author is 'the deadline'. By the end of 1998 Xaar, for one, may have qualified for 'greatness'. To paraphrase that famous quote: 'a month is a long time in racing!'

If this book errs on the side of colour, entertainment and popularity on the part of the subject, I can only beg the reader's forbearance.

Although horses from America, Canada, Australia, New Zealand, France, Italy and Hungary are included, the main bulk are from the British Isles. This is easily explained. Britain and Ireland are the cradle of the thoroughbred. Almost all overseas bloodlines – and notably contemporary American thoroughbreds – trace back to British foundations.

And who was 'The Greatest'? It is a question that no mortal being will ever be able to answer. If God were a racegoer . . .

FLAT
RACING

ALCIDE

Foaled 1955, Bay • Trained in England

Alcide was one of the best horses this century not to win the Derby. His failure to do so was almost certainly no fault of his own. Fate decreed that he was foaled during the worst era of doping and nobbling since the First World War.

Alcide, by Alycidon, was owned and bred by Sir Humphrey de Trafford, a tall and immaculately dressed member of the still hugely autocratic Jockey Club. He was trained by the equally dapper and distinguished Captain (eventually Sir) Cecil Boyd Rochfort.

He was the classic 'high mettled' racehorse. On the gallops he was forever dancing and rearing, so much so that his jockey Harry Carr described him as the most difficult colt to manage and the quickest in his movements that he had ever ridden. Yet on the racecourse, by contrast, he was lazy and lethargic, like his sire Alycidon, until he and no one else decided it was time to go. As a two-year-old Alcide won the Horris Hill Stakes at Newbury by a length and a half, coming from last to first. Inevitably he was much discussed as a Derby prospect during the winter.

I remember vividly his reappearance as a three-year-old. It was my first ever visit to Sandown Park, on what is now Whitbread Gold Cup day. Alcide, already backed for the Derby, was 11-8 on for the Royal Stakes (1¼ miles) but, tenderly ridden by Harry Carr, he was beaten a short head by the pounce of Lester Piggott on the Queen's Snow Cat. It was a touch of typical Piggott genius. Ten days later Alcide won the Chester Vase, although conspicuously unsuited by the course; and then thriving on his racing, he ran away with the Lingfield Derby Trial by twelve lengths.

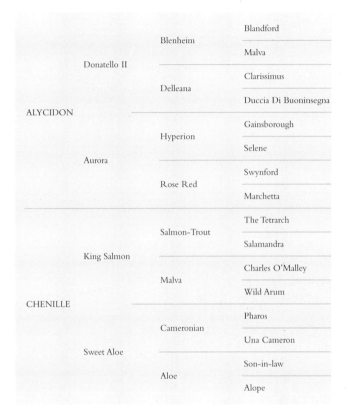

By now Alcide was a very warm favourite for the Derby and the bookmakers were beginning to quake. There are two conflicting versions of what happened next. According to Harry Carr in his autobiography, *Queen's Jockey*, Alcide was so well in himself eight days after Lingfield that he was turning himself inside-out. After playing the fool all morning, he finally gave a violent buck upwards and sideways. That evening at stables there was a large swelling on his nearside back ribs. The Derby was now out of the question. Harry Carr's view was that he must have wrenched himself internally and pulled a muscle.

Alcide's finest hour – from last to first in the straight to beat
Gladness (Garnet Bougoure) by two lengths in the King George.
Within hours Harry Carr was in hospital with acute kidney trouble.

The opinion of assistant trainer Bruce Hobbs (later a leading trainer himself) was quite different. 'In my view there is no doubt that he was "got at",' he told me years later. 'He had clearly been given a vicious blow and he was in such pain he could hardly move. He was hot favourite and the nobblers had done for him.' Three months later Alcide reappeared in the Great Voltigeur Stakes and won in brilliant style by twelve lengths.

The St Leger looked to be a formality and so it proved. Starting at 9-4 on, Alcide ran his usual lethargic race, until suddenly in the straight he decided to 'go', and won by a spectacular eight lengths.

As a four-year-old Alcide went from strength to strength – until two weeks before his main target, the Gold Cup. Alcide sustained a rapped joint and missed two or three vital gallops while Harry Carr was admitted to hospital for the removal of kidney stones, a jockey's most painful disability.

Following this entirely unsuitable preparation, Alcide was pipped by a short head by the French colt Wallaby II (Freddie Palmer) in a ding-dong finish.

Harry Carr was still in extreme discomfort five weeks later when Alcide reverted to a mile and a half in the King George VI & Queen Elizabeth Stakes. It was to be Alcide's last race, and many doubted the wisdom of 'coming back' a mile with the Leger winner. In the event Alcide proved himself a great champion, coming from last to first in the straight to beat Gladness by two lengths.

Ironically his two main targets, the Derby and the Gold Cup, had eluded him. In every other respect he was a true 'great'.

BIG RACES WON

St Leger	1958
King George VI & Queen Elizabeth Stakes	1959
Chester Vase	1958
Derby Trial Stakes	1958
Great Voltigeur Stakes	1958

ALLEGED

Foaled 1974, Bay • Trained in Ireland

In the years following the Second World War, the Prix de l'Arc de Triomphe gradually became the most prestigious all-aged Flat Race in the world. It is a race that English stables have always found hard to win. With the concentration of top-class racing in England during June, July and August, the 'Arc' tends to come a month too late. Accordingly, it should be no easier for an Irish-trained horse to win the great race. The fact that Alleged did so twice earns him a place amongst the elite.

Alleged possessed an unusual background for a Vincent O'Brien-trained American-bred. Having been bought as a yearling by a certain Monty Roberts for a mere $34,000 at Keeneland in July, he was re-submitted as a two-year-old in training in California six months later. It was here that the egregious Billy McDonald bought the Hoist The Flag colt for $175,000 (a nice profit) for Robert Sangster, initially with a view to his being trained in California. However, close examination of the colt's knees suggested he would be quite unsuited to racing on dirt; so, soon after, Alleged arrived at Ballydoyle.

No one took a great deal of notice. He was weak, backward, unfurnished and rather plain. Even Vincent and his marvellous staff found it difficult to build any condition on to him. Nonetheless, in November Alleged duly won his first and only two-year-old race by eight lengths.

The following season – the year of The Minstrel – Alleged won on his reappearance, but didn't impress. Accordingly, in his next race, the Royal Whip, he started outsider of Vincent's three runners in the race, at 33-1 – and staggered the stable by beating the 5-4 favourite Valinsky – ridden by Lester Piggott!

But still Vincent did not hurry and overface the rather gangly colt. While The Minstrel was winning the Derby, Vincent was 'thinking' an autumn campaign for Alleged. It began in staggering style with a seven-length all-the-way win in the Great Voltigeur Stakes at York. Runner-up was Classic Example, who had run The Minstrel to less than two lengths in the Irish Derby.

Alleged now looked the best three-year-old colt in Europe – and a 'certainty' for the St Leger for which he started 7-4 on. The Leger proved to be the only defeat of Alleged's career. Lester was accused of falling for a 'sucker

			Tenerani
		Ribot	
	Tom Rolfe		Romanella
			Roman
		Pocahontas II	
			How
HOIST THE FLAG (USA)			Man O'War
		War Admiral	
	Wavy Navy		Brushup
			Tourbillon
		Triomphe	
			Melibee
			Prince Rose
		Princequillo	
	Prince John		Cosquilla
			Count Fleet
		Not Afraid	
PRINCESS POUT (USA)			Banish Fear
			Alibhai
		Determine	
	Determined Lady		Koubis
			War Admiral
		Tumbling	
			Up the Hill

punch' when Dunfermline's pacemaker 'died' half a mile from home leaving Lester in front. In the event Willie Carson came with a flourish on Dunfermline and Alleged had little time to fight back. As so often was the case, a month later Lester became Dr Jekyll again in the Arc, dictating the race and launching Alleged to a brilliant success in the straight.

Alleged, now valued at $10 million, remained in training as a four-year-old, but again, as so often happens, everything went wrong. The ground was firm; he jarred his knees – and lost his action. Then came the virus that ravaged the yard. All the while the big four-year-old races were slipping away like leaves from a tree.

Finally, in the autumn, he came right. After a brilliant trial in the Prix du Prince d'Orange (track record), Alleged returned for his second Arc. It was easier than the first. Only Tantième and Ribot, since the war, had won two Arcs. Alleged retired with a syndication value of $13 million. It was Billy McDonald's finest hour!

BIG RACES WON

Prix de l'Arc de Triomphe (twice)	1977-78
Great Voltigeur Stakes	1977
Royal Whip (twice)	1977-78
Gallinule Stakes	1977

Alleged (Lester Piggott) in his first Arc triumph.

ALLEZ FRANCE

Foaled 1970, Bay • Trained in France

One of the foremost guidelines in racing is to give a horse a good name. After all, you do not find Derby winners called 'Hellcatmudwrestler'! No name could have appealed more to Parisian *turfistes* than 'Allez France' – and like a true patriot the filly came up with the goods.

Allez France was a charming filly and most feminine in appearance. Owned by the international art historian M. Daniel Wildenstein, Allez France was trained at Chantilly, first by Albert Klimscha, and latterly by the brilliant Argentinian-born Angel Penna. Penna had an affinity with fillies that was uncanny. If something disturbed him he would sit up all night to study a filly's every move. So it was with Allez France, whom he took over in 1974.

Already handled skilfully by the Scandinavian-born Klimscha, she had won the French 1000 Guineas, French Oaks (beating Dahlia by two-and-a-half lengths) and Prix Vermeille in her Classic season. Inevitably she was a firm favourite for the Prix de l'Arc de Triomphe, but was no match for the Piggott-ridden Rheingold.

Facing the normally difficult task of training a four-year-old filly, Penna responded by guiding her through the season unbeaten, an achievement climaxed by the filly's success, by a head at 2-1 on, in the Prix de l'Arc de Triomphe. Yves Saint-Martin, who had injured a thigh a week previously, was passed fit only at the twelfth hour. It was an occasion filled with Gallic emotion.

Allez France remained in training as a five-year-old, and continued to prosper although by the autumn her magic was on the wane. In the Arc she could finish only fifth to the 119-1 shot Star Appeal, while in the Champion Stakes she

			Polynesian
		Native Dancer	
	Dan Cupid		Geisha
			Sickle
		Vixenette	
			Lady Reynard
SEA BIRD II			Prince Bio
		Sicambre	
			Sif
	Sicalade		Maurepas
		Marmelade	
			Couleur
			Royal Charger
		Turn-To	
	Hail to Reason		Source Sucree
			Blue Swords
		Nothirdchance	
			Galla Colors
PRICELESS GEM (USA)			Man O'War
		War Admiral	
			Brushup
	Searching		Black Toney
		Big Hurry	
			La Troienne

was beaten one-and-a-half lengths by the three-year-old Rose Bowl.

Allez France was certainly one of the best fillies to race in France this century. In thirteen wins from twenty-one races she won £493,000, a figure only exceeded at the time by her great rival, Dahlia. However, in six meetings Dahlia never beat Allez France!

She retired to the paddocks in America, but did not prove the best of breeders. Indeed it was ten years before she bred her first winner, a useful colt called Air de France (by Seattle Slew).

'Attention, cherie!' The brilliant Argentinian horse master Angel Penna has a fatherly word with France's favourite post-war filly, Allez France.

BIG RACES WON

Prix de l'Arc de Triomphe	1974
Prix de Diane	1973
Poule d'Essai des Pouliches	1973
Prix Vermeille	1973
Prix Ganay (twice)	1974–75
Criterium des Pouliches	1972
Prix d'Ispahan	1974
Prix Dollar	1975
Prix d'Harcourt	1974

ALYCIDON

Foaled 1945, Chestnut • Trained in England

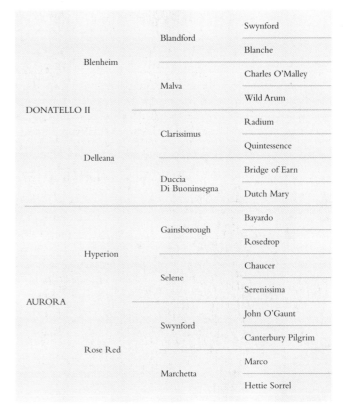

Many of the great stayers of the post-war era have shared the same characteristics – extreme laziness and a quirky nature. Alycidon, according to his jockey the five-times champion Doug Smith, was 'the greatest stayer I have ever seen and probably one of the greatest stayers of all time'.

Like so many eventual winners of the Ascot Gold Cup, Alycidon showed no inkling of ability as a two-year-old. Bred by the 17th Earl of Derby, who sadly died before his ability became apparent, Alycidon was an idle, backward 'slob'. Indeed his trainer Walter Earl found it extremely difficult to make him race-fit. In the end he devised a two-fold plan. He would work Alycidon over six or seven furlongs on the Limekilns (Newmarket's famous Summer Gallop, with wonderful spring in the turf), between two other horses leading them by a neck or half a length. If Alycidon fell behind, even by a length, he would drop everything and pull himself up. Alternatively, he would work on Lord Derby's private peat moss gallop, which ended going in the direction of the Stanley House Stables – i.e. home! With his manger in mind, Alycidon would gallop with unaccustomed enthusiasm! On the racecourse his idle nature was overcome by the fitting of blinkers, and eventually by the use of not one but two pacemakers. Thus equipped he became the first horse since Isonomy in 1879 to win the Cup 'Triple Crown' – the Gold Cup, Goodwood Cup and Doncaster Cup.

The Gold Cup in 1949 was his most evocative win. The previous autumn he had been trounced by Black Tarquin in the St Leger, after the intended pacemaker whipped round at the start leaving Alycidon to make his own running. Now, Alycidon went to battle with his two pacemakers:

Stockbridge, who led for a mile and a quarter, and Benny Lynch, who took over for the next five furlongs. Alycidon was cruising, but Black Tarquin was cantering on his heels. Doug Smith decided to go for home, gave Alycidon a back-hander and, in the words of Edgar Britt on Black Tarquin, Alycidon's quarters expanded and exploded. Alycidon won by five lengths in the most popular Gold Cup triumph since the Prince of Wales's Persimmon in 1897.

Black Tarquin, destroyed by the power of Alycidon, was never the same horse again. Five years later Chris Brasher and Chris Chataway used similar pacemaking tactics to enable Roger Bannister to run the first four-minute mile!

Alycidon was a successful stallion, but latterly a shy breeder. Alcide and Meld were his most brilliant offspring. He was destroyed painlessly in 1963. Ironically, one of his best sons, Twilight Alley, who won the Gold Cup in 1963, had identical characteristics.

A bemused Sir Noel Murless telephoned Doug Smith one evening: 'Doug – how on earth did you get that Alycidon fit? I can't get this horse to do a tap!' Doug explained the three-horse gallops on the Limekilns and suggested Sir Noel try the same system. He did: Twilight Alley won the Gold Cup and Doug was presented with a case of the finest champagne!

BIG RACES WON

Gold Cup	1949
Goodwood Cup	1949
Doncaster Cup	1949
Jockey Club Stakes	1948
Princess of Wales's Stakes	1948
Ormonde Stakes	1949

Alycidon, the first stayer since Isonomy in 1879 to win the Ascot, Goodwood and Doncaster Cup.

BAHRAM

Foaled 1932, Bay • Trained in England

It is a reasonable assertion that a horse's true merit can only be gauged by his first defeat. Therefore, any horse who retires unbeaten – leaving aside super-champions like Nearco, Ribot, Ormonde and St Simon – will always be liable to the accusation of 'he never beat a good horse'.

Such a horse was Bahram, the unbeaten winner of the Triple Crown in 1935. Bahram was bred and owned by the Aga Khan, at a time when the Imam had become by far the most substantial owner in the history of the British Turf. Between 1924 and 1937 he headed the Leading Owners' List seven times, while his breeding interests were served by five of the finest studs in Ireland. It was scarcely surprising in the circumstances that several of Bahram's leading contemporaries were also owned by the Aga Khan. This factor has been used by Bahram's detractors to diminish his achievements.

Bahram, a good-looking and powerful son of Blandford, won all of his five races as a two-year-old. In the first of them, the National Breeders' Produce Stakes at Sandown, starting at 20-1, he beat his strongly-fancied stable companion Theft (gave 9lb) by a neck. In all of his remaining two-year-old races, including the Gimcrack and Middle Stakes, Bahram started at odds-on. He headed the Two-Year-Old Free Handicap with 9st 7lb . . . just 1lb above Theft and another colt of the Aga Khan's in Hairan.

Bahram came to the 2000 Guineas without a preparatory race, having missed the Craven Stakes through being off-colour. The race resolved itself into a battle between Bahram and Theft, with Bahram running out ultimately an impressive winner by one-and-a-half lengths.

BLANDFORD	Swynford	John O'Gaunt	Isinglass
			La Flèche
		Canterbury Pilgrim	Tristan
			Pilgrimage
	Blanche	White Eagle	Gallinule
			Merry Gal
		Black Cherry	Bendigo
			Black Duchess
FRIAR'S DAUGHTER	Friar Marcus	Cicero	Cyllene
			Gas
		Prim Nun	Persimmon
			Nunsuch
	Garron Lass	Roseland	William the Third
			Electric Rose
		Concertina	St Simon
			Comic Song

Bahram became a very warm favourite for the Derby, eventually starting at 5-4. His main ante-post rivals were Hairan and Theft. The only question mark about him was his stamina. Stable confidence was high, and as Bahram went to post, Bob Lyle, the distinguished correspondent for *The Times*, reported that he had never seen a horse move better. Prince Aly Khan confessed to a friend that he had struck the biggest bet of his life!

Early in the race Freddie Fox on Bahram found himself in a very tight spot and shouted to Harry Wragg on Theft to pull over. Wragg complied and was later hauled before the

The Aga Khan is overwhelmed by congratulations as the unbeaten Bahram (Freddie Fox) returns to unsaddle after the Derby. Note the uninvited presence of tipster Ras Prince Monolulu in the background!

stewards for his pains! Bahram took the lead over two furlongs out and won in majestic style. Theft was fourth and Hairan, ridden by Gordon Richards, unplaced.

Bahram was made 11-4 on to complete the Triple Crown and did so with the greatest of ease – by five lengths. The only drama was an accident to Freddie Fox on the eve of the race. Charlie Smirke stepped in – as he did nineteen years later for the suspended Lester Piggott on Never Say Die.

The St Leger was Bahram's last race. The Aga Khan retired him to stud with eulogies of affection and a declaration that he would never sell the first Triple Crown winner since 1903.

He was a horse of magnificent presence. A favourite characteristic was for him to lean against the wall of a stable with his legs crossed, looking around him in a supercilious way. It was this studied indolence that occasionally made him less impressive than his critics demanded. But no horse beat him – nor did any extend him.

The tailpiece was sad. The Aga Khan sold him in 1940 to an American syndicate for $160,000. He never thrived in America and was eventually exported to Argentina where he died in 1956. At other times the Aga sold his Derby winners Blenheim and Mahmoud to America, and many British breeders never forgave him for the loss of three potentially great stallions. To cap this, at the start of the Second World War, the Aga sold almost all his horses in training and went to live in neutral Switzerland.

BIG RACES WON

Derby	1935
2000 Guineas	1935
St Leger	1935
St James's Palace Stakes	1935
Gimcrack Stakes	1934
Middle Park Stakes	1934

BALLYMOSS

Foaled 1954, Chestnut • Trained in Ireland

Amongst the reasons that a great horse can fail to win the Derby are injury, inability to stay the trip and extreme bad luck in running. In the case of Ballymoss the prime reason was his ill fortune to be foaled in the same year as Crepello.

Of course there was another major factor. Ballymoss was a very backward horse who despite winning two Classics did not reach his pinnacle until a four-year-old. Vincent O'Brien bought Ballymoss for 4500 guineas at the Doncaster Sales. It was early in Vincent's transition from top National Hunt trainer to Flat Racing 'wizard', and Vincent was hard on the look-out for owners. Through a mutual friend he met the American millionaire builder John McShain at Doncaster Races.

Ballymoss was a very average two-year-old, winning a minor race at Leopardstown from four starts. His reappearance in the Madrid Free Handicap was a disaster. He finished well back, and showed no enthusiasm. But the ground was heavy.

However, a month later, on good ground, he won the Trigo Stakes, beating his stable companion, the great mare Gladness, at 20-1. After a brilliant mixed gallop Vincent decided to send him to Epsom.

Crepello was a horse in 100,000 and he won the Derby with style by a length and a half. But Ballymoss at 33-1 beat the remainder comfortably and a month later, starting at 9-4 on, he won the Irish Derby with considerable ease.

Defeat in the Great Voltigeur Stakes was again blamed on soft going. I remember it well: it was a vile day and Lester Piggott, to the best of my recollection, was beaten on six fancied horses! So came the St Leger and another wet

			Phalaris
		Pharos	
			Scapa Flow
	Nearco		
			Havresac II
		Nogara	
			Catnip
MOSSBOROUGH			
			Gainsborough
		Bobsleigh	
			Toboggan
	All Moonshine		
			Chaucer
		Selene	
			Serenissima
			Bayardo
		Gainsborough	
			Rosedrop
	Singapore		
			The Tetrarch
		Tetrabbazia	
			Abbazia
INDIAN CALL			
			Sunstar
		Buchan	
			Hamoaze
	Flittemere		
			Swynford
		Keysoe	
			Keystone II

Yorkshire afternoon; spirits were in decline. But the light sandy soil at Town Moor inhibited Ballymoss far less than the bog of the Knavesmire, and Ballymoss, ridden by T. P. Burns, won by a length from Court Harwell.

As a four-year-old, Ballymoss, like Busted ten years later, became an exceptional horse. He won the Coronation Cup, Eclipse Stakes, King George VI & Queen Elizabeth Stakes and finally a dramatic Prix de l'Arc de Triomphe.

Ballymoss galloped brilliantly before the Arc and Vincent had a substantial ante-post bet. Everything had gone right. Then on the day of the race, the inevitable occurred . . . the

Ballymoss ('T. P.' Burns) overcomes soft ground to win the St Leger from Court Harwell (Scobie Breasley) and Brioche (Edward Hide).

skies opened and the rain poured down in torrents. Vincent tried desperately to cancel his bet, to no avail. Scobie Breasley, now Ballymoss's regular jockey, finished tailed off in the second race, and returned shaking his head in gloom. Viewing the recorded telecast of the race thirty years later reveals the full extent of the impact of the rain: the horses seem to come home in slow motion! But Ballymoss, now at his peak of strength and maturity, and ridden by the artistic Breasley, somehow galloped through the mud.

During his career Ballymoss won £107,165 in stakes, establishing a new UK record. He was not a great stallion, but sired one Derby winner in Royal Palace. What he did do was launch Vincent O'Brien on his Classic path.

BIG RACES WON

Prix de l'Arc de Triomphe	1958
St Leger	1957
Irish Derby	1957
King George VI & Queen Elizabeth Stakes	1958
Eclipse Stakes	1958
Coronation Cup	1958

BAYARDO

Foaled 1906, Brown • Trained in England

Bayardo was, by common consent, one of the outstanding horses of the first half of the twentieth century. Yet he was beaten in both the 2000 Guineas and the Derby. Bayardo was trained by the 'Wizard of Manton', Alec Taylor, for an awkward, irascible man named Mr A.W. Cox (whose *nom de course* was 'Mr Fairie').

Two weeks before his first appearance in the New Stakes at Royal Ascot, Otto Madden and some other jockeys travelled to Manton to ride in a trial, testing the stable's most promising two-year-olds against a three-year-old called Seedcake. Madden, riding Bayardo, won the trial easily by six lengths. One can imagine Alec Taylor's astonishment, therefore, when Madden told him on the eve of Ascot that he had accepted another ride in the New Stakes! 'I'm sorry,' stated Madden, 'but I'm afraid your two-year-olds can't be any good. That three-year-old I rode murdered them!'

'That wasn't the three-year-old, you idiot,' exclaimed Taylor. 'That was Bayardo!'

It was the costliest mistake of Madden's life, as he lost the riding of Bayardo for good. Bernard Dillon rode Bayardo as a two-year-old and the legendary Danny Maher rode him for the remainder of his career. Bayardo was unbeaten in seven races as a two-year-old, but the following spring was cold and dry and the colt's feet, which were fleshy and shelly, gave Taylor considerable worry.

Taylor was loath to run his Champion in the 2000 Guineas, but the owner insisted. Bayardo, although odds-on, finished only fourth to the King's Minoru. Two weeks before Epsom Bayardo began to thrive, but on the day interference from the favourite, Sir Martin, running down Tattenham Hill,

BAY RONALD	Hampton	Lord Clifden	Newminster	
			The Slave	
		Lady Langden	Kettledrum	
			Haricot	
	Black Duchess	Galliard	Galopin	
			Mavis	
		Black Corrie	Sterling	
			Wild Dayrell Mare	
GALICIA	Galopin	Vedette	Voltigeur	
			Mrs Ridgway	
		Flying Duchess	The Flying Dutchman	
			Merope	
	Isoletta	Isonomy	Sterling	
			Isola Bella	
		Lady Muncaster	Muncaster	
			Blue Light	

cost him all of half a dozen lengths and Maher accepted defeat. Again, King Edward VII's Minoru was the hugely popular winner.

Thereafter Bayardo went from strength to strength. Over the next fifteen months he dominated the Turf in a way that few horses have done. He won the Prince of Wales's Stakes at Royal Ascot, the Eclipse, the St Leger (annihilating Minoru), three races at Newmarket in the autumn including the Champion Stakes, and the Liverpool St Leger.

As a four-year-old he won the Chester Vase narrowly, with Maher leaving it desperately late. Bayardo had gradually

Bayardo – brilliance tempered by quirks of character.
Unbeaten as a two-year-old, he eventually won twenty-two out of twenty-five races.

become quirky and would 'plant' for lengthy periods outside his box. Furthermore, at Newmarket he would refuse to canter down in front of the stands. Accordingly, Maher would weave his way through the coaches and carriages in the car-park, much to Bayardo's amusement.

It was this quirkiness that persuaded Maher to believe that ...yardo did not care to be in front for too long. Hence his ... at Chester. In the Ascot Gold Cup, however, Bayardo ... .iis way to the front six furlongs from home to win ... pleased by four lengths, thus affording much delight to ...ie critics of Maher's tactics.

Maher had his 'revenge', however, in Bayardo's final race, the Goodwood Cup. Starting at 20-1 on, Maher allowed the three-year-old Magic (receiving 36lb) almost a furlong's start, and failed by a neck to catch the younger horse.

Bayardo retired the winner of twenty-two of his twenty-five races. Sadly, he died at the age of eleven following a thrombosis, but his stud influence was considerable with his grandson Hyperion becoming one of the great prepotent stallions.

BIG RACES WON

St Leger	1909
Gold Cup	1910
Eclipse Stakes	1909
Champion Stakes	1909
Prince of Wales's Stakes	1909
Liverpool St Leger	1909
Chester Vase	1910
Middle Park Plate	1908
Dewhurst Plate	1908

BRANTOME

Foaled 1931, Bay • Trained in France

BLANDFORD	Swynford	John O'Gaunt	Isinglass
			La Flèche
		Canterbury Pilgrim	Tristan
			Pilgrimage
	Blanche	White Eagle	Gallinule
			Merry Gal
		Black Cherry	Bendigo
			Black Duchess
VITAMINE	Clarissimus	Radium	Bend Or
			Taia
		Quintessence	St Frusquin
			Margarine
	Viridiflora	Sans Souci II	Le Roi Soleil
			Sanctimony
		Rose Nini	Le Sancy
			Rosewood

Once upon a time – up to thirty years ago – the Ascot Gold Cup was considered the ultimate target of a four-year-old's career. Nowadays, sadly, the position is quite the reverse. To win a Gold Cup is a positive stigma for a potential stallion, and indeed, until Classic Cliche's success in 1996, no English Classic winner had won the Gold Cup since the War.

It was very different between the wars when the criterion of excellence in a thoroughbred was the ability to win over five furlongs as a two-year-old, and up to two-and-a-half miles as a four-year-old. Such a horse was Brantome, owned, bred and raced by Baron Edouard de Rothschild in France. A son of one of this century's greatest stallions, Blandford – sire of four Derby winners in seven years – Brantome was unbeaten in four races as a two-year-old, including the French Two-Year-Old 'Triple Crown', the Prix Robert Papin, Prix Morny and Grand Criterium. He was rated 7lb clear of his nearest rival, Admiral Drake, in the French Free Handicap.

His three-year-old season was interrupted severely by a persistent cough, which prevented him from running in both the French Derby and the Grand Prix de Paris. Nonetheless, he began the year by winning the French 2000 Guineas (at 10-1 on), and Prix Lupin – and ended it by winning the French St Leger and Prix de l'Arc de Triomphe, in brilliant style.

As a four-year-old, his target was duly made the Ascot Gold Cup. On the way he triumphed in the Prix du Cadran – the French equivalent – in record time for the race, and *turfistes* on both sides of the Channel looked forward to one of the great races for the Gold Cup, between Brantome and Windsor Lad.

Two things went wrong, however. Windsor Lad, the 1934 Derby winner, and also a son of Blandford, was withdrawn from the race by his owner, the bookmaker Mr Martin Benson, for fear of defeat. Then, eleven days before the race, Brantome got loose and galloped down the main street at Chantilly. Although he skilfully avoided several cars, he lost three shoes and sustained an unpleasant cut before he was caught. His injury kept him off work for four days and his trip to Ascot was about to be abandoned. However, his sporting owner insisted upon running – and Brantome was beaten for the first time. When the news reached France no one was prepared to believe that he had finished out of the first three.

Brantome was never the same after Ascot, although he did win the Prix du Prince d'Orange at Longchamp in the autumn. But his record of twelve wins with over two million francs, from five furlongs – two-and-a-half miles – established him as one of the great French horses this century. But for his accident, he would probably never have been beaten.

BIG RACES WON

Poule d'Essai des Poulains	1934
Prix Royal Oak	1934
Prix de l'Arc de Triomphe	1934
Prix du Cadran	1935
Prix Lupin	1934
Prix Robert Papin	1933
Prix Morny	1933
Grand Criterium	1933

Brantome returns after winning the Prix du Cadran (the French Gold Cup) in record time.

BRIGADIER GERARD

Foaled 1968, Bay • Trained in England

Ask a dozen 'experts' their formula for breeding a great horse and you will probably receive a dozen different answers. 'Breed the best to the best – and hope for the best!' is the traditional formula, but it was not a method approved by Brigadier Gerard's breeder and part-owner John Hislop.

To breed his champion, John sent a shy-breeding mare of medium-class pedigree to Queen's Hussar, a relatively unfashionable stallion whose nomination fee had dropped to 200 guineas. (I recall this fact vividly as I also sent a mare to Queen's Hussar in 1967, and bred a foal so moderate his name escapes me!) The result, nonetheless, to John's everlasting credit, was one of the greatest horses of the post-war era, who won his first sixteen races.

John Hislop, former champion amateur jockey, journalist, breeding expert and adviser, and company director, excelled in many areas of horse racing. But he was never, on his own admission, a rich man. It was fortunate, therefore, that before 'The Brigadier' went into training as a yearling, his wife Jean had made him promise never to sell their cherished colt.

I recall having tea with Desmond and Molly Baring (The Brigadier's granddam, Brazen Molly, was allegedly named after my hostess) on the day that the powerful colt had won his third race, the Washington Singer Stakes. 'What did you think of him?' asked Molly, having heard me commentate on the race on BBC TV. 'I think he's good,' I replied. 'They've been offered £60,000 for him,' said Molly. 'I think they should take it!' I replied. To their credit they didn't, nor did they accept an offer of £250,000 before the 2000 Guineas, nor did they accept a genuine 'blank' cheque later in his career!

QUEEN'S HUSSAR	March Past	Petition	Fair Trial
			Art Paper
		Marcelette	William of Valence
			Permavon
	Jojo	Vilmorin	Gold Bridge
			Queen of the Meadows
		Fairy Jane	Fair Trial
			Light Tackle
LA PAIVA	Prince Chevalier	Prince Rose	Rose Prince
			Indolence
		Chevalerie	Abbot's Speed
			Kassala
	Brazen Molly	Horus (GB)	Papyrus
			Lady Peregrine
		Molly Adare	Phalaris
			Molly Desmond

It was one of nature's ironic jokes that Brigadier Gerard was foaled in the same year as Mill Reef and My Swallow. The three of them composed the nucleus of possibly the finest field for the 2000 Guineas since the War. Mill Reef had won the Greenham Stakes in a common canter by four lengths; while My Swallow had beaten a useful horse owned by the author called Midnight Cowboy with equal ease at Kempton.

The press and public considered the 2000 Guineas a two-horse race. Only the late Clive Graham in the *Daily Express* tipped The Brigadier. Brigadier Gerard did not just win, he went past his rivals as if they were standing still, to win by

three lengths. At the time it was impossible to believe the result: I was convinced that Mill Reef had failed to 'run his race' – either because he was off-colour, or because the giant, coltish Minsky had frightened and intimidated him in the pre-parade ring. Mill Reef was never beaten again – which to a degree justified my beliefs – and sadly the two great horses never met again.

Brigadier Gerard did not run in the Derby because his owner believed he would not stay. So the opportunity for a re-match did not materialize until the following year on August 15th – in the Benson & Hedges Gold Cup.

Infuriatingly, six days before the race Mill Reef pulled a muscle in his quarters and was withdrawn. Worse was to follow: The Brigadier, after fifteen straight wins, was defeated by the enigmatic Roberto. Ridden by the Panamanian Braulio Baeza after Lester Piggott had declined the ride, the Derby winner made every yard of the running in record time. It was The Brigadier's only defeat.

He retired at the end of the season with a record comparable to the very best. Only two Classic winners this century (Pretty Polly and Bayardo) have won more races. He was a truly great champion.

BIG RACES WON

2000 Guineas	1971
King George VI & Queen Elizabeth Stakes	1972
Eclipse Stakes	1972
Champion Stakes (twice)	1971-72
Sussex Stakes	1971
Queen Elizabeth II Stakes (twice)	1971-72
St James's Palace Stakes	1971
Prince of Wales's Stakes	1972
Lockinge Stakes	1972
Middle Park Stakes	1970

OPPOSITE: Brigadier Gerard, winner of his first fifteen races, including the 2000 Guineas, Eclipse and King George VI & Queen Elizabeth Stakes.

BROWN JACK

Foaled 1924, Brown • Trained in England

It is a fact of racing life that the public have a deeper affection for the jumping, year-to-year horses like Arkle, Sea Pigeon and Red Rum than for the Flat Racing 'stars' who retire to stud after just two seasons' racing.

Brown Jack was probably the most popular flat-race horse this century. Yet ironically, in complete reversal of the normal trend, he began life as a hurdler – and then became a flat-race 'crack'! Brown Jack, by Jackdaw, was bred in Ireland by Mr George Webb, who sent him to Goff's Sales as a yearling in August 1925 – without his eliciting a single bid! After two private sales he was bought as a backward three-year-old in training for £750 by the Hon. Aubrey Hastings, with a long-term objective of winning the Champion Hurdle for his patron Sir Harold Wernher.

Despite starting his jumping career at Bournemouth and being viewed with a lack of interest verging on contempt by the lads in the yard, Brown Jack progressed throughout the season and went to Cheltenham for the Champion Hurdle a well-fancied 4-1 chance. It was only the second year of the Challenge Cup with a prize of just £680, but Brown Jack achieved the remarkable feat of winning the 'Hurdlers' Derby' within seven months of jumping his first hurdle. Watching the race was the ten times champion flat-race jockey Steve Donaghue, who declared to Hastings after the race: 'He'll win on the Flat – and I'll ride him'. Thus, remarkably, ended Brown Jack's hurdling career – and began a memorable chapter of Flat Racing history.

For the next seven seasons Brown Jack, ridden by Donoghue, never missed the Royal Ascot meeting. Within three months of winning the Champion Hurdle, he was handicapped with

7st 13lb in the Ascot Stakes – and won. In 1929 he was beaten a short head in the Ascot Stakes by Old Orkney – and three days later won the Queen Alexandra Stakes by four lengths.

In May 1929 Aubrey Hastings had died, but with the Wroughton stable taken over by his assistant, Ivor Anthony, everything went on as before. In 1930 Brown Jack was unplaced in the Ascot Stakes – and once again won the Queen Alexandra Stakes three days later, beating his great rival Old Orkney. This pattern was repeated in 1931.

By now Brown Jack's popularity was immense, and his reception compared with that of a Derby winner. In 1932

			Orme
		Missel Thrush	
	Thrush		Throstle
			Charibert
		Chemistry	
JACKDAW			Retort
			St Simon
		St Frusquin	
	Sakuntala		Isabel
			Muncaster
		Ashdown	
			Miss Maria
			Arbitrator
		Kilwarlin	
	Kroonstad		Hasty Girl
			St Simon
		Sabra	
QUERQUIDELLA			Belinda
			Gallinule
		Wildfowler	
	Garganey		Tragedy
			Buckingham
		Sapphire	
			Eastern Rose

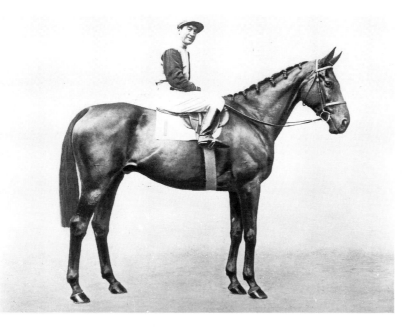

Brown Jack and Steve Donoghue – the most popular and successful Royal Ascot combination this century.

he ran in the Gold Vase (unplaced) prior to his fourth success in the Queen Alexandra, while the following year the stable settled for just one foray – and won number five in the 2 miles 6 furlong marathon.

In 1934, at the age of ten, he went to Ascot for the seventh and final time – and for the first time since 1930, started odds against for 'his' race – indeed at one stage 3-1 was offered. The *Evening Standard* banners read simply: 'BROWN JACK TODAY'. Ivor Anthony was too nervous to watch the race and sat in the paddock under a tree. It was an epic race. Brown Jack and Solarium drew clear in the straight. Slowly, inch by inch, and then foot by foot, Brown Jack and Donoghue forged to the front to cheers the like of which had never been heard before. Afterwards there were scenes unprecedented at Ascot. Strong men wept unashamedly: reserved old ladies gathered their skirts and ran to the Unsaddling Enclosure; hats were thrown in the air. It was a fitting end to a remarkable career which also included

a Doncaster Cup and a win and four seconds in the Goodwood Cup.

Gelded as a yearling, Brown Jack was kind, but idiosyncratic: lazy on the gallops, but like a lion on the racecourse. Steve Donaghue, the horseman supreme, loved him like no other horse – and he loved Donoghue. On their final photocall, Brown Jack pushed his head forward and licked Steve's face from ear to ear.

BIG RACES WON

Goodwood Cup	1930
Doncaster Cup	1930
Queen Alexandra Stakes (six times)	1929-34
Ascot Stakes	1928
Chester Cup	1931
Ebor Handicap	1931
Champion Hurdle	1928

CARBINE

Foaled 1885, Bay • Trained in Australia

It takes a very special racehorse for his name to become part of the language. Such a horse was Carbine, who won the Melbourne Cup under a remarkable 10st 5lb. Ever since that famous day, Australian poker players have called two pairs of 'tens' and 'fives' a 'Carbine'!

Carbine was bred in New Zealand by two English expatriate parents, Musket and Mersey. Musket was lucky to be alive. His eccentric owner-breeder, Lord Glasgow, was so unimpressed by him as a foal that he ordered him to be shot. Happily for all concerned, John Osborne, the stable jockey, pleaded for his life and Musket's salvation was clinched when Lord Glasgow died in March 1869. In 1878, after a successful racing career, but limited success at stud, Musket was exported to New Zealand where he was bred initially to half-bred mares. Eventually, he changed hands again and Carbine was foaled in 1885.

Carbine's career was extraordinary by any standards. Unbeaten as a two-year-old in New Zealand, he travelled to race for the superior prize money in Australia as a three-year-old. Unfortunately for his owner Dan O'Brien, Carbine was given an appalling ride by a jockey called Derrett in the V. R. C. Derby at Flemington, with the result that O'Brien offered him for sale – quite possibly to recoup gambling debts. He changed hands for 3000 guineas.

Thereafter Carbine scarcely looked back. At the Randwick Sydney Cup Meeting, he was beaten in the A.J.C. Autumn Plate (1½ miles) on the first day; won the Sydney Cup (2 miles) on the second day; and then won the All-Aged Stakes (1 mile), the Cumberland Stakes (1¼ miles) and the A.J.C. Plate (2¼ miles) at the same meeting!

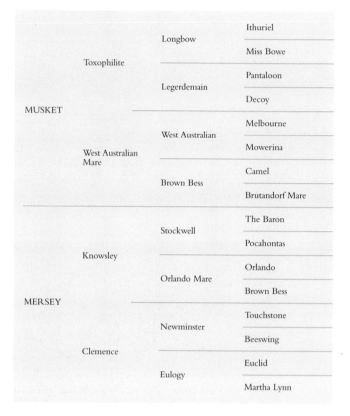

As a four-year-old he was campaigned in a similar manner, culminating this time in winning all of his five races at the four-day Sydney Cup meeting! It was, however, as a five-year-old that he reached his zenith, notably with his remarkable Melbourne Cup triumph. Carrying 10st 5lb in a record-sized field of thirty-nine, he won Australia's greatest race in the then fastest-ever time of 3 minutes 28.25 seconds. The runner-up Highborn, receiving 53lb, later won the Sydney Cup under 9st 3lb. Not even Phar Lap's success in 1930 evoked greater scenes of enthusiasm.

In the autumn Carbine was retired with a career record of forty-three races, thirty-three wins, six seconds and three thirds. A bay horse, standing 15.3hh, he had a rather plain head with an unusual jagged white stripe. He made little impact at stud in Australia, but in 1895 the Duke of Portland acquired him to stand alongside St Simon at his Welbeck Abbey Stud in Nottinghamshire. Despite the worst slump in Australia's history, 2000 horse players stood at the docks to wave Carbine farewell.

Happily, Carbine justified his purchase by siring Spearmint, who went on to win the 1906 Derby. One hundred years on, Australia has only ever seen one comparable horse: Phar Lap.

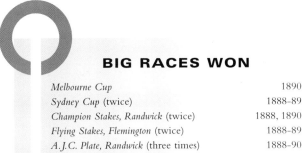

BIG RACES WON

Melbourne Cup	1890
Sydney Cup (twice)	1888-89
Champion Stakes, Randwick (twice)	1888, 1890
Flying Stakes, Flemington (twice)	1888-89
A.J.C. Plate, Randwick (three times)	1888-90

Plain, stocky and short-backed he may have been, but Carbine became a legend in Australia and New Zealand.

CIGAR

Foaled 1990, Bay • Trained in USA

The story of Cigar, the American 'World Champion' of the 1990s, brings into sharp focus the huge gulf between racing on 'dirt'– the standard surface in the States – and racing on grass.

For 300 years, England has been the cradle of the thoroughbred and racing has traditionally taken place on turf. The framework of racing in America, with racing meetings lasting for several weeks, lends itself to the use of an artificial surface. Hence almost all of America's great races are run on 'dirt'. The style of racing and the medication permitted to 'patch up' unsound horses represents a total antithesis to the disciplined conformity of racing in Britain.

Cigar, between October 1994 and July 1996, gained immortality by winning sixteen successive races. Only the great Citation had achieved a comparable sequence. All sixteen wins were gained on 'dirt'. The sequence began in the autumn of his four-year-old career. His previous eleven races were on turf. He had won just one.

Cigar was foaled at the Country Life Farm in Maryland, owned by the aviation billionaire Allan Paulson. His sire, Palace Music, had raced successfully in Europe, where he won the Champion Stakes, and America, while his dam, Solar Slew, by Seattle Slew, was the most expensive two-year-old filly of her generation, at $510,000. She was, however, a disappointment on the track, and failed to win in seven starts.

Cigar, who eventually stood 16.3hh, was big and backward as a yearling and, after throwing a curb midsummer, was freeze-fired and given time to mature. His first race was in February of his three-year-old season. He ran over six

PALACE MUSIC (USA)	The Minstrel (CAN)	Northern Dancer	Nearctic
			Natalma
		Fleur (USA)	Victoria Park
			Flaming Page
	Come My Prince (USA)	Prince John	Princequillo
			Not Afraid
		Come Hither Look	Turn-To
			Mumtaz
SOLAR SLEW (USA)	Seattle Slew (USA)	Bold Reasoning (USA)	Boldnesian
			Reason to Earn
		My Charmer (USA)	Poker (USA)
			Fair Charmer (USA)
	Gold Sun (ARG)	Solazo	Beau Max
			Solar System
		Jungle Queen	Claro
			Agrippine

furlongs at Santa Anita and finished a modest seventh of nine. He won his second race – on 'dirt' at Hollywood Park – but in the next nineteen months, racing on grass, he gained only one further success. He was troubled by sore shins and inflamed hocks, and there was regularly heat evident in his knees. At the end of his three-year-old season he underwent arthroscopic surgery on both knees and had a bone chip removed.

The following spring he was switched to the East Coast of America and the stable of Bill Mott. Madelaine Paulson, a former flight attendant and Allan's third wife, was now

Cigar (Jerry Bailey) completes a sensational unbeaten season in the 1995 Breeders' Cup Classic at Belmont Park.

managing Cigar and believed that the more yielding race-tracks of the East would suit Cigar's style of galloping. But when Cigar resumed racing in July his performance remained frustrating . . . until he switched to racing on 'dirt'.

Many will wonder why it took so long to make the decision. It finally happened at Aqueduct, New York, on October 28th. Cigar won by eight lengths. Suddenly the coaster was rolling. Four weeks later he was elevated from a modest allowance race to the Grade 1 NYRA Mile. Cigar exploded. He won by seven lengths. A star was born.

It was the following season – Cigar was now five – that saw him attain the perfect score of ten wins out of ten, a record matched only once in the previous sixty years. Jerry Bailey had grabbed the ride and stuck with him for the remaining fifteen races of his now sensational career.

His first three wins of the year were at Gulfstream Park in Florida. The third, the $500,000 Gulfstream Park Handicap, which he won by seven-and-a-half lengths, saw one of the most impressive performances of his career. Oaklawn Park, Pimlico and Suffolk Downs followed. At Allan Paulson's request he was flown back to the West Coast for the Hollywood Gold Cup. The locals, locked into a view that he was a 'talking horse' who had 'got lucky' in the East, opposed him. Cigar bolted in by three-and-a-half lengths.

His autumn campaign was spectacular: the Woodward, the Jockey Club Gold Cup (against the Kentucky Derby winner Thunder Gulch) and the $3 million Breeders' Cup Classic. Now Cigar was a megastar worldwide.

When Sheikh Mohammed al Maktoum conceived the Dubai World Cup, to be run in the desert the following spring with a prize of $4 million, Cigar had to be there, or it wouldn't work. Cigar was there, but he arrived on the back of a foot problem. After a tough journey across the Atlantic,

he did not eat, and in Dubai he was not permitted to race with the coagulent lasix. It was a famous race and for a brief moment it looked as if Cigar might be beaten by the Californian horse Soul of the Matter. But Cigar thrust his head back in front to win by half a length.

Sadly for Cigar's connections, the target of a record seventeen straight wins was not achieved. Cigar was beaten comfortably by Dare And Go in the Pacific Classic at Del Mar. But he had done enough to attract a bid of $30 million from a Japanese stud. It was turned down. Six months later those Japanese were mildly relieved when Cigar was found to be firing blank bullets in the Stallion Barn.

So in the end was it justifiable to call Cigar a World Champion racehorse? In my opinion the answer is no. Sure, he was nigh unbeatable on that glutinous 'dirt' surface. But he cut a pretty modest figure on the turf.

BIG RACES WON

Dubai World Cup	1996
Breeders' Cup Classic	1995
Arlington Citation Challenge	1996
Hollywood Gold Cup	1995
Jockey Club Gold Cup	1995
Woodward Stakes (twice)	1995, 1996
Oaklawn Handicap	1995
Pimlico Special Handicap	1995
Gulfstream Park Handicap	1995

CITATION

Foaled 1945, Bay • Trained in USA

One of the key assets in racing horses – as in gambling – is knowing when to stop. Nowadays owners are widely criticised for 'packing off' horses to stud too early in their careers. But only those closest to a horse can assess, with reasonable accuracy, when a horse's decline is imminent.

Citation was a horse who should almost certainly have retired at the end of his three-year-old career. Bred by the baking powder tycoon Warren Wright's Calumet Farm, Citation was a mature two-year-old, winning eight of his nine races, worth $115,690. His only defeat was at the hands of his stable companion, the brilliant filly Bewitch, in the Washington Park Futurity.

In his Classic season, Citation was almost unbeatable. He won nineteen of his twenty races, worth $709,470 – at the time a record sum for seasonal earnings. His only defeat came at the hands of a three-year-old called Saggy, over six furlongs, at Havre de Grace. Various reasons were put forward for this reverse, notably that he was carried wide on the final bend, and that Eddie Arcaro had not ridden him before. (His previous rider, Al Snider, had been drowned on a fishing trip off the Florida Keys.) The truth is that his outstanding trainer, Ben Jones, had almost certainly left him a gallop 'short' – as was his habit – after a six-week absence from the track.

His Triple Crown was achieved in brilliant style. He won the Kentucky Derby by three-and-a-half lengths from his outstanding stable companion Coaltown; the Preakness by five-and-a-half lengths, and the Belmont by eight lengths. So little did the Classics tax him that in between he fitted in the Jersey Stakes at Garden State, New Jersey, which he won by eleven lengths in record time.

			Ajax
		Teddy	
	Bull Dog		Rondeau
			Spearmint
		Plucky Liege	
BULL LEA			Concertina
			Voter
		Ballot	
	Rose Leaves		Cerito
			Trenton
		Colonial	
			Thankful Blossom
			Bayardo
		Gainsborough	
	Hyperion		Rosedrop
			Chaucer
		Selene	
HYDROPLANE			Serenissima
			Marcovil
		Hurry On	
	Toboggan		Tout Suite
			St Simon
		Glacier	
			Glasalt

In the autumn, Citation was sent to California in a bid to surpass Stymie's record career earnings of $918,485, but after two wins which took him to within $50,000 of the target, he 'popped' an osselet, and was sent home to Kentucky to be bar-fired.

If Citation had been retired to stud at that point, he would now be regarded as one of the three great American colts this century, along with Man O'War and Secretariat. Sadly, however, his owners were obsessed with two racing landmarks. Firstly, Stymie's elusive record, and secondly, the alluring $1 million mark. So Citation returned to action thirteen months later, as a five-year-old, and immediately ran into a formidable opponent in Noor. For the next four months Noor inflicted defeat after defeat on Citation, initially in receipt of 22lb, and finally *giving* Citation 1lb. Citation finished second in seven out of eight races. After a further injury Citation returned to the track ten months later at the age of six, and eventually struck a winning run which took him past the 'magical million'.

Citation, a medium-sized horse by the Calumet stallion Bull Lea, out of a Hyperion mare bought from Lord Derby, rightly became a legend in American racing – and is commemorated by a life-size statue at Hialeah Park. But nowadays I wonder – should he have raced beyond the age of three . . .?

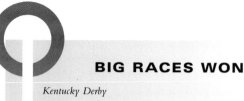

BIG RACES WON

Kentucky Derby	1948
Preakness Stakes	1948
Belmont Stakes	1948
Gold Cup (Belmont)	1948
Jockey Club Gold Cup	1948
American Derby	1948
Jersey Stakes	1948
Flamingo Stakes	1948
Hollywood Gold Cup	1951

Citation (Eddie Arcaro), winner of nineteen of his twenty races as a three-year-old, including the American Triple Crown.

COLOMBO

Foaled 1931, Bay • Trained in England

Colombo, up until 1986, enjoyed the doubtful distinction of being regarded the unluckiest loser of the Derby this century. It is my view, however, that in the television age this myth would never have been perpetuated.

Colombo, a bay horse by Manna, was bought for a bargain 510 guineas, as a yearling, on behalf of the shipping magnate Lord Glanely. He won all of his seven two-year-old races, including the New Stakes, Richmond Stakes and Imperial Breeders' Produce Stakes, and was clear top-weight in the Free Handicap with 9st 7lb. Some journalists were already calling him 'Horse of the Century'.

During the autumn his owner, a large, mercurial man with a thick walrus moustache, and dubbed by the racing public 'Old Guts and Gaiters', had negotiated to retain the Australian-born, French-based jockey Rae Johnstone for 1934.

Colombo won the Craven Stakes with ease, and in the 2000 Guineas started the shortest-priced favourite for forty years at 7-2 on. Colombo won by a length from Easton, but was far from spectacular. Nonetheless the racing world believed that only two factors could prevent Colombo from winning the Derby: either if he failed to stay, or if Rae Johnstone – who had served a two-year suspension in Australia for 'stopping' a horse for betting purposes – prevented him from winning. Johnstone, on his own subsequent admission, was offered £10,000 – a fortune in those days – to do just that.

Despite the doubts, Colombo went off favourite at 11-8. The dangers were considered to be Umidwar (H. Wragg), Windsor Lad (C. Smirke), Easton (G. Richards), and Brantome's number two in France, Admiral Drake (E. C. Elliott). What happened in the race has been discussed ever since. Johnstone was tight on the rails running down Tattenham Hill, with Steve Donoghue in front of him and Smirke and Gordon Richards on his 'outer'. For some reason Johnstone didn't shout for room, which with his mount now beaten, Donoghue claims he would have given. So Colombo had to wait until well into the straight and then pull out to the wide outside. A furlong out Windsor Lad, Easton and Colombo were almost in line. The crowd roared themselves hoarse. But suddenly Colombo faltered, was beaten, and Windsor Lad forged away to win for Charlie Smirke.

In my view, had 'live' television existed, with expert

				Cyllene
MANNA	Phalaris	Polymelus		Maid Marian
		Bromus	Sainfoin	
			Cheery	
	Waffles	Buckwheat	Martagon	
			Sesame	
		Lady Mischief	St Simon	
			Vain Duchess	
LADY NAIRNE	Chaucer	St Simon	Galopin	
			St Angela	
		Canterbury Pilgrim	Tristan	
			Pilgrimage	
	Lammermuir	Sunstar	Sundridge	
			Doris	
		Montem	Ladas	
			Kermesse	

Colombo (Rae Johnstone) returns to scale after his 2000 Guineas success at 7–2 on.

analysts, as today, Johnstone would have been exonerated, and Colombo branded a non-stayer. Steve Donoghue, who had hoped to ride Colombo until Johnstone came on the scene, did not help to ease the pain. 'Had I ridden him he would have won on the bit by lengths,' he stated.

On June 29th, after Colombo had been beaten at Royal Ascot at 5-1 on, Rae Johnstone was on his way back to France. For a generation of racegoers, the 1934 Derby was the race that Colombo and Rae Johnstone *lost* . . .

BIG RACES WON

2000 Guineas	1934
Craven Stakes	1934
New Stakes	1933
National Breeders' Produce Stakes	1933
Richmond Stakes	1933
Imperial Produce Stakes	1933

CREPELLO

Foaled 1954, Chestnut • Trained in England

		Blandford	Swynford
	Blenheim		Blanche
		Malva	Charles O'Malley
DONATELLO II			Wild Arum
		Clarissimus	Radium
	Delleana		Quintessence
		Duccia Di Buoninsegna	Bridge of Earn
			Dutch Mary
		Massine	Consols
	Mieuxce		Mauri
		L'Olivete	Opott
CREPUSCULE			Jonicole
		Solario	Gainsborough
	Red Sunset		Sun Worship
		Dulce II	Asterus
			Dorina

Crepello was almost certainly one of the outstanding Derby winners this century. For many years Lester Piggott stated categorically that he was the best horse he had ever ridden. But sadly the strong, handsome 16.2½hh colt never had the opportunity to show the extent of his greatness.

Crepello was owned and bred by the late Sir Victor Sassoon, who was seventy-five years old when Crepello began to race. With much of his year spent abroad, Sir Victor always liked to have runners at Royal Ascot. The trainer, Noel Murless, with little else available and against his judgement, ran the backward Crepello in the Windsor Castle Stakes. The ground was firm and Crepello, always straight in front, was far from ready for a hard race. Tenderly ridden by Lester Piggott, he was beaten a short head by Fulfer.

A week later Murless felt a tiny notch on Crepello's suspensory ligament. The great trainer hated anyone other than himself to touch his horses' legs so he ordered a cloth bandage, known as a 'Newmarket cloth', to be sewn on each of Crepello's forelegs. He wore them throughout his career – and all that time the leg, on such a fine horse, was a worry to Murless. Crepello did not run again until the autumn, when he finished fourth to Pipe of Peace in the Middle Park Stakes and then won the Dewhurst Stakes comfortably.

In the spring of 1957, Murless took a rare step. Never much of a bettor, he took odds of 66-1 to £100 that Crepello would win the 2000 Guineas and Derby. After a dry spring and firm ground, Crepello went to the 2000 Guineas without a preliminary race. Held together beautifully by Lester Piggott,

he struck the front 200 yards out and won comfortably by half a length.

Crepello was now firm favourite for the Derby and galloped brilliantly, but the combination of firm ground and the threat of 'nobblers' caused him to ease in the market to 11-4. On the day, however, he hardened to 6-4 and again, superbly ridden by Piggott, he swept past Ballymoss to win by a length and a half.

Sadly, it was to be his last race. He was withdrawn on the morning of the King George VI & Queen Elizabeth Stakes after a downpour had made the ground soft and false; and then, whilst in training for the St Leger, his tendons finally showed signs of strain and he was retired to stud. Only Piggott and Murless have an inkling as to how good Crepello was. With his legs in mind, Piggott never really let him down, so he was never fully extended.

Busted apart, Crepello proved a better sire of fillies and broodmares than of colts. He was certainly a great racehorse – and trained by an equally great trainer.

BIG RACES WON

Derby	1957
2000 Guineas	1957
Dewhurst Stakes	1956

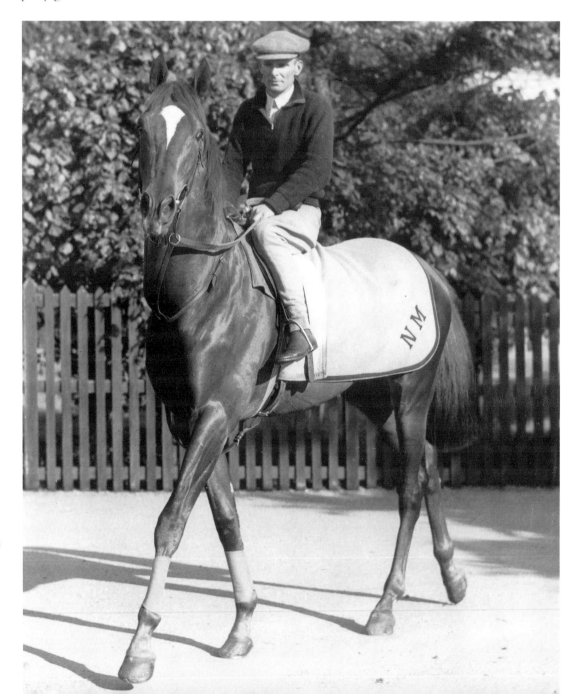

Crepello, the tall but striking winner of the 1957 2000 Guineas and Derby. Note the 'Newmarket cloths' that he always wore after his first race.

DAHLIA

Foaled 1970, Chestnut • Trained in France

Just as 1968 had seen the birth of two great colts in Mill Reef and Brigadier Gerard, 1970 produced two of the great post-war fillies in Allez France and Dahlia.

They were formidable rivals, and bear fascinating comparison:

– Dahlia never beat Allez France in six encounters – but won £497,741, a record for a European horse.

– Allez France never won outside of France. Dahlia won in France, England, Ireland, Canada and the USA.

– Allez France was consistent and won thirteen of her twenty-one races. Dahlia never bloomed until June or July and ran many indifferent races.

Dahlia was tough, and at her best was spectacularly brilliant. Her success in the 1973 King George VI & Queen Elizabeth Stakes was one of the most staggering big-race victories I have ever seen. Last with half a mile to race, she swept past a field that included Rheingold and Roberto to win by six lengths going away. A week earlier Dahlia had beaten the four-lengths Oaks winner Mysterious by three lengths in the Irish Oaks – a result which, at the time, nobody believed!

After an injury-affected autumn, Dahlia went to America for the Washington International and showed her love of travel by winning easily from Big Spruce. She failed to win until July as a four-year-old, and along the way jockey Bill Pyers was sacked.

Lester Piggott teamed up with the mare in the King George and the Benson & Hedges Gold Cup, and won both comfortably. Once again an American autumn campaign was planned and she duly won the Man O'War Stakes and

				Hyperion
		Aureole		Angelola
	Vienna			Turkhan
		Turkish Blood		Rusk
VAGUELY NOBLE				Pharos
		Nearco		Nogara
	Noble Lassie			Big Game
		Belle Sauvage		Tropical Sun
		Alibhai		Hyperion
				Teresina
	Honeys Alibi			Beau Pere
		Honeymoon		Panoramic
CHARMING ALIBI				Abjer
		Hierocles		Loika
	Adorada II			Gallant Fox
		Gilded Wave		Ondulation

Canadian International Championship before meeting with defeat in the Washington International.

Dahlia was again 'cold' in the spring of 1975 and Piggott was temporarily given the 'sack'. But she came good to win a second Benson & Hedges before tailing right off in the autumn and retiring to stud.

Dahlia was trained with a mixture of volatility, genius and inspiration by Maurice Zilber for the Texan oil and metals magnate Nelson Bunker Hunt. Unlike Allez France, she proved a success at stud, foaling a dual Group 1 winner in Dahar (by Lyphard), and a Group 3 winner in Rivlia (by Riverman).

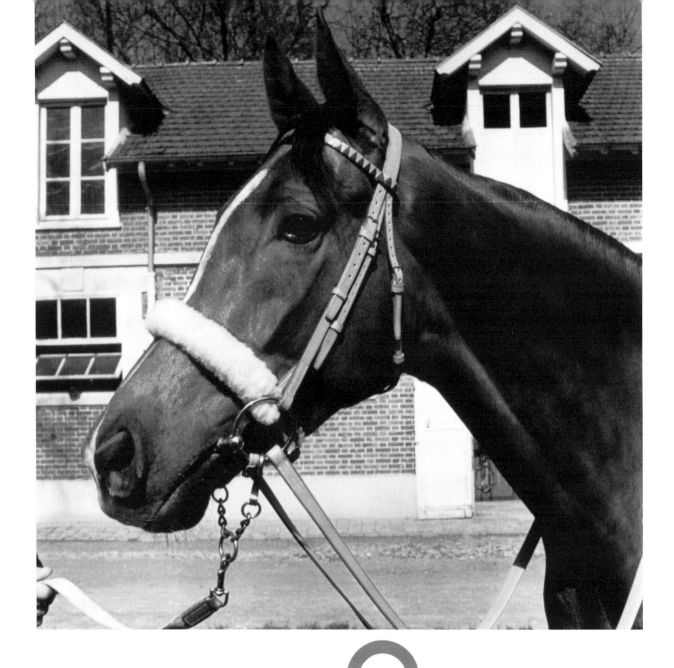

Dahlia, the twentieth century Marco Polo (female variety!)
– winner of $497,741 in France, England, Ireland, Canada and the USA.

BIG RACES WON

Irish Guinness Oaks	1973
King George VI & Queen Elizabeth Stakes (twice)	1973-74
Benson & Hedges Gold Cup (twice)	1974-75
Grand Prix de Saint Cloud	1974
Prix Saint-Alary	1973
Man O'War Stakes	1974
Canadian International Championship	1974
Washington D.C. International	1973

DANCING BRAVE

Foaled 1983, Bay • Trained in England

In April 1985, after Walter Swinburn had been suspended for a riding offence at Epsom, I observed on TV: 'It has always been a mystery to me why the world's greatest Flat Race should be run on one of the worst racecourses'. Considerable comment was engendered by the remark, with the popular riposte: 'Well the best horse nearly always wins; you've never seen a *great* horse beaten in the Derby . . .'

It was ironic, therefore, that a year later just such a situation came about. Dancing Brave could certainly be compared with any of the great horses of the past thirty years – but he lost the Derby.

A medium-sized bay horse by Lyphard, Dancing Brave ran just twice as a two-year-old, winning minor races over a mile at Sandown and Newmarket. After overcoming soft ground in the Craven Stakes and winning comfortably by a length, he started 15-8 favourite for the 2000 Guineas, despite never having beaten an opponent of quality. His performance, however, was spectacular, brilliant acceleration enabling him to win by three lengths from the Free Handicap winner Green Desert.

His trainer, Guy Harwood, now had to decide whether to restrict him to one mile – or take a chance on his stamina in the Derby. Encouraged by his jockey, Greville Starkey, who made a public statement shortly before the race that 'The Brave' was 'bomb-proof', and was 'sure to win', Harwood grasped the nettle and sent his star colt to Epsom.

As with Colombo's Derby, the race will be argued about for many years, and, as with Colombo, the jockey received the blame! Starkey was accused of setting The Brave an impossible task. It was my view at the time, and remains so, that Dancing

			Nearco
		Nearctic	
	Northern Dancer		Lady Angela
			Native Dancer
		Natalma	
LYPHARD (USA)			Almahmoud
			Fair Trial
		Court Martial	
	Goofed		Instantaneous
			Formor
		Barra II	
			La Favorite
			Turn-To
		Sir Gaylord	
	Drone		Somethingroyal
			Tom Fool
		Cap and Bells	
NAVAJO PRINCESS (USA)			Ghazni
			Matrice
	Pago Pago	
	Olmec (USA)		Pompilia
			Beau Max
		Chocolate Beau	
			Otra

Brave was beaten because he hung inwards when his rider wanted to improve his position. He continued to 'lean in' well into the straight; and by the time that Starkey had pulled him out, balanced him, and launched him, it was just too late. Shahrastani held on by a rapidly diminishing half length.

It was Dancing Brave's only defeat in Europe. He won the Eclipse Stakes by four lengths and the King George (ridden by Eddery) by a diminishing three parts of a length, confirming that he barely stayed a mile and a half.

His autumn campaign was directed towards the Prix de l'Arc de Triomphe where, ridden again by Eddery, he came

Dancing Brave (Pat Eddery) shows brilliant acceleration to win one of the finest Arc de Triomphes
in the history of the race from Bering (Gary Moore) and Triptych (Angel Cordero).

alarmingly late to win in brilliant style, and record time, from one of the strongest fields since the War.

Dancing Brave was almost the complete racehorse. He had speed, acceleration and he stayed (just) a mile and a half. He was blessed, too, with a perfect temperament. He retired to stud at Newmarket with a valuation of £14 million, but after limited success was exported to Japan in 1991.

BIG RACES WON

2000 Guineas	1986
King George VI & Queen Elizabeth Diamond Stakes	1986
Eclipse Stakes	1986
Prix de l'Arc de Triomphe	1986
Craven Stakes	1986

DANTE

Foaled 1942, Brown • Trained in England

Dante, who was bred and raced by Sir Eric Ohlson of Belvedere, Scarborough, was the only northern-trained horse to win the Derby in the past 100 years.

He was also a classic example of the role of fate in racing. In 1941, Sir Eric bought his dam, Rosy Legend, from the sale of the late Lord Furness's bloodstock for 3500 guineas. The foal, a brown colt by Nearco, was sent by Sir Eric to the Yearling Sales, but failed to reach a reserve of 3500 guineas. Sent into training with Matt Peacock at Middleham, Yorkshire, the Nearco colt remained 'on offer' throughout the autumn, but failed to find a buyer. So the reluctant Sir Eric was compelled to race Dante – and soon realised his good fortune.

Dante won all his six two-year-old races, ending up with the Middle Park Stakes. He headed the Free Handicap with 9st 7lb, 1lb ahead of the Manton-trained Court Martial. Already an idol in the North of England, he reappeared at wartime Stockton, and was so impressive in appearance and performance that he started even money favourite for the 2000 Guineas. To the dismay of the whole of Yorkshire, however, he was beaten a neck by Court Martial. Two days before the race, Dante had appeared to be suffering from impaired vision and it was thought that he had been struck in the eye by a flint. Court Martial challenged on his 'blind' side, and Dante's rally came all too late.

The 1945 Derby was run for a final time at Newmarket, as Epsom was not yet in a state of repair – although the war had been over for a month. With Court Martial unlikely to stay, Dante, ridden by Willie Nevett, was made favourite at 100-30 and duly won by two lengths from Midas, with Court

Martial a further neck away third. The North of England treated the result like a second V. E. Day: the famous Middleham bell tolled, and at the Dante Ball 'Cock of the North' Nevett was carried shoulder-high.

Dante was now an odds-on favourite to complete the Triple Crown on Yorkshire soil, and the bookmakers had colossal liabilities. However, in August disturbing rumours began to circulate as to Dante's well-being. As late as August 22nd there were firm denials from the stable that anything was amiss, but on August 25th Dante was scratched – and was never to race again. It transpired that, far from suffering

				Polymelus
		Phalaris		Bromus
	Pharos			Chaucer
		Scapa Flow		Anchora
NEARCO				Rabelais
		Havresac II		Hors Concours
	Nogara			Spearmint
		Catnip		Sibola
				Bay Ronald
		Dark Ronald		Darkie
	Dark Legend			Amphion
		Golden Legend		St Lucre
ROSY LEGEND				St Frusquin
		St Just		Justitia
	Rosy Cheeks			Gallinule
		Purity		Sanctimony

A. G. Haigh's portrait of Dante, painted in the year of his Derby triumph.

a physical injury, Dante was the victim of a far more serious eye disease which eventually left him entirely blind.

Whatever the rights and wrongs of the affair, the deception created a scandal which left deep scars for years to come. Happily, Dante's ocular disability was not hereditary, and he sired two Classic winners in Darius and The Queen's Carrozza.

BIG RACES WON

Derby (wartime)	1945
2000 Guineas (wartime)	1945
Middle Park Stakes	1944
Coventry Stakes	1944

ECLIPSE

Foaled 1764, Chestnut • Trained in England

Eclipse, whose name is borne by the oldest Group 1 mile-and-a-quarter flat race, was the first truly great racehorse.

A grandson of the Darley Arabian, he was bred by William, Duke of Cumberland, at Windsor Forest. On the Duke's death in 1765, he was bought by a Smithfield meat salesman called William Wildman for seventy-five guineas. A massively-built lengthy chestnut colt with a white stocking on his off-hind leg, Eclipse was so temperamental as a young horse that his owner considered gelding him. To have done so would have undermined the entire future of the Stud Book over the next 200 years!

Eclipse did not race until he was five, when Wildman took him to Epsom for a £50 Plate to be run in three four-mile heats. The course began in the region of Lord Derby's house, The Oaks, and would finish on the Downs. He won the first heat easily, whereupon the legendary Irish gambler Colonel Dennis O'Kelly bet that he could place all five runners in the second heat in the correct order. The bet was accepted, and O'Kelly stated that his forecast was: 'Eclipse first, and the rest nowhere!' – meaning that Eclipse would finish a distance (240 yards) in front of his rivals. Eclipse did so and O'Kelly collected. . . . A month later, O'Kelly bought a half-share in Eclipse for 650 guineas, and eventually the other half for 1000 guineas, after a game of chance over the price.

Under O'Kelly's guidance, Eclipse became a legend. He was never beaten, and never extended, in eighteen races. Indeed he was so vastly superior to any possible rival it was almost impossible to make a match for him. It was said that Eclipse could run a mile in a minute – a claim that casts serious doubts upon the accuracy of reporting at the time!

Eclipse was the sire of three of the first five winners of the Derby, and almost all the great horses of the twentieth century trace back to him. On his death his anatomy was examined in detail by an eminent young French veterinarian whose paper on the subject was largely responsible for the foundation of the Royal Veterinary College of London. His purpose had been to determine the reasons for Eclipse's amazing speed, generally attributed to his exceptional heart-room. Eclipse's skeleton was eventually re-assembled, and now stands in the National Horse Racing Museum in Newmarket.

Eclipse, in full stride – the famous Sartorius oil painting.

EPINARD

Foaled 1920, Chestnut • Trained in France

When the French produce a good horse he is often very good indeed, and Epinard most definitely comes into that category. Jack Leach, ex-jockey, author and journalist, described him as the most fascinating horse he had seen. 'He was fantastic,' he wrote.

Epinard was owned and bred by M. Pierre Wertheimer, whose family still race in Paris. Recent Arc winners in Ivanjica and Gold River have carried the Wertheimer colours.

As a yearling, Epinard did not impress his breeder and he was almost sold. Eventually, however, he was sent into training with Eugene Leigh, a French-based American.

He began his two-year-old career at Deauville in the Prix Yacowlef which he won by five lengths, in a canter from what Willie Pratt – one of the leading French trainers of the time – considered his best two-year-old. In the Prix Morny, however, he was hopelessly left, and met with his only defeat over the next fourteen months. His remaining two-year-old races included the Grand Criterium, Criterium de Maisons-Laffitte and the Prix de la Forêt, all of which he won in magnificent style.

By now he was considered one of the best two-year-olds ever seen in France. Because his owner-breeder had thought so little of him as a foal, he had not been entered in the Prix du Jockey Club (the French Derby). None-theless, he began his three-year-old career with four impressive wins. It was now that the plan took shape to send him to England. At first the Royal Hunt Cup was chosen, but after consideration the stable decided to send a 'sighter' in the five-year-old Select. The Stewards Cup –

in those days a race of colossal prestige, and a major gambling medium – was chosen for Epinard. He was given 8st 6lb by the handicapper – more than any three-year-old had ever carried to victory. Nonetheless, Epinard was backed from 33-1 to 7-2 and, ridden by the American Everett Haynes, he staggered his rivals by winning in a canter by two lengths.

Epinard travelled back to France a national hero, but returned to England in the autumn facing another 'impossible' task. This time he was set 9st 2lb in the Cambridgeshire. Only Foxhall, forty-two years earlier, had won the great race

BADAJOZ	Gost	Callistrate	Cambyse
			Citronelle
		Georgina	Trocadero
			Gladia
	Selected	Raeburn	St Simon
			Mowerina
		Il Segreto	Chevron
			Nameless
EPINE BLANCHE	Rock Sand	Sainfoin	Springfield
			Sanda
		Roquebrune	St Simon
			St Marguerite
	White Thorn	Nasturtium	Watercress
			Margerique
		Thorn Blossom	Martenhurst
			Eye Sweet

with 9st as a three-year-old. The going was firm in France, and Epinard was prepared at Singleton, near Goodwood. In the last week he was stabled at Newmarket. This is where Jack Leach comes into the story. According to Leach, he rode in a gallop in the week of the race, over seven furlongs on racecourse side – and noticed that Epinard was working over a mile on a parallel gallop. It seemed to Leach that the two groups of horses jumped off at the almost identical moment – with Epinard a furlong behind Leach's group. Leach writes in his book *Sods I Have Cut On The Turf*: 'We jumped off and came a good gallop. As we passed Felix [his brother], Epinard was with us. In fact he pulled up in the bunch as if he had been with us all the way. I have never been so astonished in my life . . .!'

Epinard started favourite at 3-1 for the Cambridgeshire, but his rider had been persuaded to tack over to the stands rails from his high draw. He did so violently, seemingly six lengths clear, and never gave his mount a breather throughout. He was caught and beaten in the last strides by Michael Beary riding the Earl of Coventry's filly Verdict, carrying 7st 12lb. The following season Verdict won the Coronation Cup! Epinard received an astonishing reception. Leach concludes: 'Epinard was a horse and a half, and the gamest runner I ever saw!'

Epinard (Everett Haynes) – his name means 'spinach'
. . . but he was no 'Popeye'.

BIG RACES WON

Prix d'Ispahan	1923
Grand Criterium	1922
Prix de la Forêt	1922
Criterium de Maisons-Laffitte	1922
Stewards Cup	1923